The Mayflower Compact

CORNERSTONES OF FREEDOM

SECOND SERIES

Melissa Whitcraft

Children's Press®
A Division of Scholastic Inc.
New York • Toronto • London • Auckland • Sydney
Mexico City • New Delhi • Hong Kong
Danbury, Connecticut

Photographs © 2003: Art Resource, NY: 4 bottom (Foto Marburg), 8 top (Image Select); Bridgeman Art Library International Ltd., London/New York: cover bottom (Library of Congress, Washington DC), 23 (New York Historical Society), 5 left (Prado, Madrid, Spain), 25, 29, 45 bottom left (Private Collections), 3 (Royal Geographical Society, London, UK), 5 right, 44 top left (Thyssen-Bornemisza Colletion); Brown Brothers: 37; Corbis Images: 7 top, 9 bottom, 10, 12, 17 bottom, 22, 27 left, 30 bottom, 38, 44 top right (Bettmann), 6 (Burstein Collection), 26 (James Marshall), 30 top (Gunter Marx), 8 bottom (Reuters NewMedia Inc.), 28 (David H. Wells), 21; Getty Images/Eyewire Collection: 20; Hulton|Archive/Getty Images: 17 top, 19 left, 24, 45 top left; North Wind Picture Archives: 4 top, 35, 44 bottom (N. Carter), cover top, 9 top, 11, 15, 19 right, 33, 34, 36, 39 right, 39 left, 40, 45 right; Pilgrim Hall Museum, Plymouth, MA: 27 right.

XNR Productions: Map on page 7

Library of Congress Cataloging-in-Publication Data

Whitcraft, Melissa.

The Mayflower Compact / Melissa Whitcraft.

p. cm. — (Cornerstones of freedom. Second series)

Summary: Discusses the Pilgrims' voyage to Plymouth, Massachusetts, and the colony they established after their arrival, aided by Native Americans and governed by an agreement called the Mayflower Compact. Includes bibliographical references and index.

ISBN 0-516-24203-2

1. Mayflower Compact (1620)—Juvenile literature. 2. Pilgrims (New Plymouth Colony)—Juvenile literature. 3. Mayflower (Ship)—Juvenile literature. 4. Massachusetts—History—New Plymouth, 1620–1691—Juvenile literature. [1. Mayflower Compact (1620) 2. Pilgrims (New Plymouth Colony) 3. Mayflower (Ship) 4. Indians of North America—Massachusetts. 5. Massachusetts—History—New Plymouth, 1620-1691.] I. Title. II. Series.

F68 .W57 2003

974.4'8202—dc21

2002009029

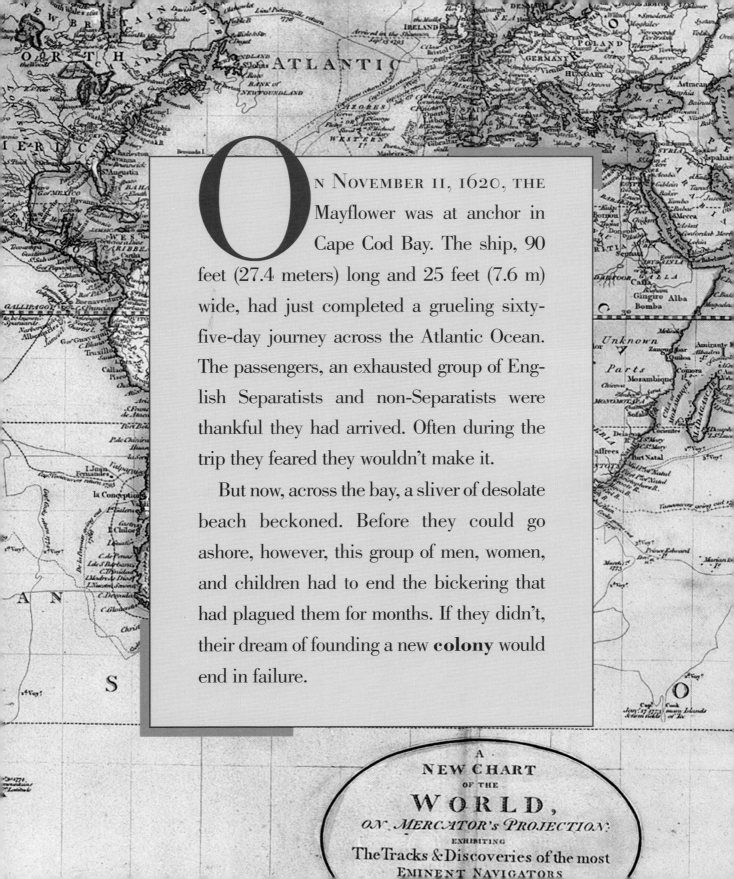

ON November 11, 1620, the Mayflower was at anchor in Cape Cod Bay. The ship, 90 feet (27.4 meters) long and 25 feet (7.6 m) wide, had just completed a grueling sixty-five-day journey across the Atlantic Ocean. The passengers, an exhausted group of English Separatists and non-Separatists were thankful they had arrived. Often during the trip they feared they wouldn't make it.

But now, across the bay, a sliver of desolate beach beckoned. Before they could go ashore, however, this group of men, women, and children had to end the bickering that had plagued them for months. If they didn't, their dream of founding a new **colony** would end in failure.

A
NEW CHART
OF THE
WORLD,
ON MERCATOR's PROJECTION:
EXHIBITING
The Tracks & Discoveries of the most
EMINENT NAVIGATORS

Originally founded as a monastery in 1052, Westminster Abbey was rebuilt between the thirteenth and sixteenth centuries. Since the Protestant Reformation it has served as the seat for the Anglican Church in England.

In 1517 the German priest Martin Luther started the Protestant Reformation when he hammered a list of 95 complaints againt the Catholic Church to a church door.

THE SEPARATISTS

The Separatists had instigated this hazardous voyage. Founded in 1606, they were a small **sect** of English Protestants. Protestants were European Christians who first "protested" against some of the practices of the Roman Catholic Church in the 1500s. Their movement became known as the Protestant Reformation. The Protestants criticized the Catholic Church because they believed the Bible, not the Pope, was the only source of truth for learning about God. By setting up their own **denominations,** these early Protestants hoped to reform Christianity.

When the Separatists arrived in Cape Cod Bay, they hoped to establish a religious community that was "separate" from the Church of England. Founded in 1534 by King Henry VIII, the Church of England, or Anglican Church, was a Protestant church.

To the Separatists, however, the Church of England was still too similar to the Catholic Church. The King controlled all the Anglican churches in England, just as the Pope controlled all the Catholic churches throughout Europe. Separatists believed that each individual church should be in charge of its own congregation. In addition, Catholics and Anglicans based their religious services on lavish ceremonies. Separatists believed that

King James I of England did not appreciate the opinions of the Separatists.

HENRY VIII AND THE CHURCH OF ENGLAND

Henry VIII broke with the Catholic Church because he wanted to divorce his first wife to marry a second. When the Pope refused to grant the divorce, King Henry started a church that he, not the Pope, could control.

King Henry VIII (1491–1547) married and divorced six times during his reign.

the best way to practice Christianity and understand God's will was to study the Bible.

James I was the king of England at the time the Separatists came into existence. Their opinions infuriated him. Like most kings, James I did not want his subjects criticizing him. He worried that if he let these Separatists complain about the Church of England, they would soon start complaining about the way he ran the country.

To avoid his anger, the Separatists worshiped secretly in the home of William Brewster, who had once been an Anglican minister. However, the threat of **persecution** and prison always hung over them. By 1609 the Separatists knew they had to leave England. Under the leadership of Brewster, John Robinson, and John Carver, the group moved to Protestant Holland and settled in the cloth-manufacturing city of Leiden.

"THEY KNEW THEY WERE PILGRIMS"

In 1618 the Separatists had to move again. They were having difficulty earning enough money to survive. Their children were being drawn into Dutch society. They were forgetting their English heritage and the importance of their own religious upbringing. The community had to find a

William Brewster realized the Separatists had to leave England in order to practice their religion without fear.

Afraid of what the future might bring, the Pilgrims put their faith in God.

Despite its history of war with Catholic Spain, Protestant Holland was known to be tolerant of other religions.

In 1497, the Italian navigator John Cabot, sailing for the English, explored the coast of Newfoundland and Nova Scotia.

place to live where outside influences would not threaten them.

After much discussion, the Separatists decided to **emigrate** to North America in the **"New World."** They knew about North America because English sea captains had explored its Atlantic coast since 1497. In 1602, eighteen years before the *Mayflower* voyage, Bartholomew Gosnold sailed into Cape Cod Bay. Giving both Cape Cod and Martha's Vineyard their English names, Gosnold returned home with exciting descriptions of ocean waters full of fish.

The Separatists chose to settle just south of the Hudson River. This region was the northernmost border of the

The geographic coastline of Martha's Vineyard has not changed significantly since Batholomew Gosnold first saw it in 1602.

English territory, under the jurisdiction, or legal control, of the London Virginia Company. Having chosen an area, they still had to find a **sponsor.** The Separatists were not wealthy enough to finance the trip themselves.

Eventually a group of English merchants, or business-men, agreed to fund their expedition. In return for this financial support, the Separatists agreed to pay off the debt by shipping back grain and **natural resources** such as beaver **pelts,** fish, and lumber. The merchants would then sell these goods for a **profit.**

When the time came to leave Holland for England, where the Separatists would begin their long voyage aboard the *Mayflower,* there was still not enough money for all of them to go. John Robinson, the minister, stayed with some wives and children. John Carver, a successful businessman, went. So did

The French explorer Samuel De Champlain was also interested in the "New World." In 1608 he founded a settlement on the St. Lawrence River in Quebec.

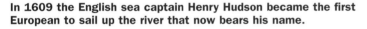

In 1609 the English sea captain Henry Hudson became the first European to sail up the river that now bears his name.

SETTLING NORTH AMERICA

English colonists had to have the king's permission to settle in North America, and they could only settle in areas controlled by English **trade** organizations. In 1620 the London Virginia Company ran the English territory that stretched from present-day New Jersey to North Carolina.

William Bradford's book,
Of Plimoth Plantation,
is a great source of
information about the
history of the Pilgrims.

Brewster and his ward, or dependent, William Bradford.

Bradford became one of the colony's most influential leaders. He served as governor thirty times between 1621 and his death in 1657. He also wrote a detailed history of the community, *Of Plimoth Plantation,* which was published in 1646. "Plimoth" with an *I* and no *U,* the old English spelling of "Plymouth," still appears often in the title of current editions of the book.

In the book Bradford described the departure from Leiden to England on July 22, 1620, as heartbreaking. The Separatists were going out into the unknown. No one knew what would happen. All were afraid, but none thought of turning back. As Bradford wrote, "they knew they were pilgrims" and having faith in God they "lifted up their eyes to the heavens."

SETTING OUT

Once at the port of Southampton, England, the Separatists met with unexpected delays. Thomas Weston, the spokesman for the investing merchants, had recruited additional colonists. The Separatists were suspicious of these Strangers, as they called them. They were not part of their religious community. They were, however, similar to the Separatists. Both groups were made up mostly of poor farmers who were looking for a new start.

* * * *

Whatever their religious differences, the Strangers' presence also caused a space problem. Additional Separatists were to follow the *Mayflower* on a smaller ship, the *Speedwell*. But the Separatists discovered that the *Speedwell* leaked and therefore could not make the journey. Since Strangers were now on the *Mayflower*, some Separatists had to be left behind.

Further complications occurred when Weston announced that the investors had changed the contract. Both the Separatists and the Strangers had agreed to pay off their debt in seven years, with the understanding that their houses and personal garden plots would belong to them. They also

THE PILGRIMS

A pilgrim is anyone who takes a journey for religious reasons. Bradford described the Separatists as "pilgrims" because they were traveling to North America to establish a new religious colony. Today, all early settlers in Plymouth, including the *Mayflower* Strangers, are known as Pilgrims.

One of the early manuscript pages from *Of Plimoth Plantation*

FACSIMILE OF FIRST PAGE OF GOVERNOR BRADFORD'S "HISTORY OF THE PLIMOTH PLANTATION"

11

The weather was fair when the *Mayflower* started its voyage. However, soon the ship was battling fierce winds and high seas.

believed that they would get a portion of the funds raised from the goods they shipped back to England.

Weston now demanded all profits from these sales go entirely to the investors. He also stated that all houses and gardens would belong to them. Both the Strangers and the Separatists refused to sign the new agreement before leaving England. Eventually Weston would get their signatures, but the disagreement created a lasting animosity, or hatred, between the colonists and Weston.

THE VOYAGE

The *Mayflower,* captained by Christopher Jones, finally set sail on September 6, 1620. On board were 102 passengers. Only 37 were part of the original group that lived in Leiden. Small compartments built onto the front and back of the deck provided accommodations for the captain, officers, crew, and some Pilgrim leaders. The rest had to make do with whatever space they found in the lower part of the ship.

Conditions here were terrible—dark, wet, and foul-smelling. But the deck, stacked with supplies, was not safe. Violent northern gales made the situation worse. Bradford noted that "in . . . these storms the winds were so fierce and the seas so high" that Captain Jones often had to pull down the sails and let the *Mayflower* ride out the storm on its own.

These conditions were a source of constant friction. The Separatists believed God sent the bad weather because the Strangers did not follow their faith. The Strangers believed that God was angry because the Separatists had left the Church of England. The crew blamed all the passengers. Their disorganization had caused the *Mayflower* to leave later than scheduled. Therefore, instead of sailing before the autumn storms, the ship had to sail through them.

As dangerous as the trip was, only one passenger and one sailor died. A boy was born and was named, appropriately, Oceanus. By journey's end the new colonists were in a terrible state. Weakened by a bad diet, seasickness, and the cold, damp weather, many regretted the decision to leave England.

However, when they saw land on November 9, they laughed and cried at their good fortune. As Bradford noted, "after long beating at sea . . . they were not a little joyful." The first trial was over, but there were more to come.

ARRIVAL

The weather had blown the *Mayflower* 300 miles (482 km) off course. The colonists had to decide whether to continue down the coast or settle in what the English called New England. With winter fast approaching, they chose to stay.

The decision created a new set of problems. If the *Mayflower* sank on the way back to England, how would Weston know where to send the remaining Separatists and much-needed supplies? In addition, the Pilgrims worried about the isolation. There were a few scattered English settlements in the Virginia territory. On Cape Cod there were none. The Plymouth Virginia Company, which was supposed

For weeks the *Mayflower* struggled through the autumn storms of the Atlantic.

to manage England's territory from present-day Maine to New York, had failed to establish any communities.

The nearest English communities were temporary fishing villages on the coast of Maine. Here, at the edge of the sea with thick forests behind them, the settlers would be on their own.

There was also the issue of **civil order.** Since the Pilgrims were settling outside land governed by the king, they were not subject to English law. Therefore, they had to write their own laws. How could they do that when they continually argued with each other?

The solution came in a letter their minister, John Robinson, had sent with them. In his message he instructed the Separatists to do what was necessary to elect leaders who would "entirely love and . . . diligently promote the common good" of the new colony. Encouraged by these words, the Separatist leaders came up with a brief document they labeled the "Association and Agreement."

THE MAYFLOWER COMPACT

Today, the Association and Agreement is called the Mayflower Compact. It stated that all who signed it agreed to come together "into a Civil Body Politic." It also stated that this Body Politic would write "just and equal laws . . . for the general good of the Colony."

Because the colony was first and foremost a religious community, the Mayflower Compact also stated that those who signed the agreement would work "for the glory of God." The Separatists wanted their settlement to reflect what they thought God expected of them.

In addition, the Mayflower Compact acknowledged that those "whose names [were] underwritten" were "loyal subjects of our sovereign Lord, King James." Even though the Separatists wanted freedom to practice their religion in peace, they still thought of themselves as loyal Englishmen.

After weeks of tension, the Separatists and Strangers put differences aside and signed the Mayflower Compact.

The signatures of some of the men who signed the Mayflower Compact

Here is the original document in its entirety. Notice the differences in spelling between then and today, and the use of the word "ye" in place of the word "the."

THE MAYFLOWER COMPACT

In ye name of God Amen. We whose names are underwriten, the loyall subjects of our dread soveraigne Lord King James, by ye grace of God, of great Britaine, franc, & Ireland king, defender of ye faith, &c.

Haveing undertaken, for ye glorie of God, and advancemente of ye christian faith, and honour of our king & countrie, a voyage to plant ye first colonie in ye Northerne parts of Virginia, doe by these presents solemnly & mutualy in ye presence of God, and one of another, covenant & combine our selves togeather into a civill body politick; for our better ordering & preservation & furtherance of ye ends aforesaid; and by vertue hearof, to enacte, constitute, and frame shuch just & equall lawes, ordinances, Acts, constitutions, & offices, from time to time, as shall be thought most meete & convenient for ye generall good of ye colonie: unto which we promise all due submission and obedience.

In witnes whereof we have hereunder subscribed our names at Cap-Codd ye 11 of November, in ye year of ye raigne of our soveraigne Lord king James of England, france, & Ireland ye eighteenth and of Scotland ye fiftie fourth. Ano: Dom. 1620.

John Carver, who is thought to have written the Compact, was the first Separatist to sign. Then came the others. Miles Standish, a former soldier, was the first Stranger to add his name. Other Strangers followed. In the end, forty-one men accepted the agreement. No women signed because they had no legal rights.

A wise leader, John Carver understood the importance of having a good relationship with local Native Americans.

Although he was not a Separatist, Miles Standish became a valuable and respected member of the Pilgrim colony.

WHERE IS THE AGREEMENT TODAY?

The original document is lost. Seventeenth-century copies of the Mayflower Compact appear in Bradford's *Of Plimouth Plantation* and Nathaniel Morton's *New England Memorial*.

When they first arrived, the Pilgrims explored forests filled with birch, oak, and maple trees.

★ ★ ★ ★

The signers unanimously chose John Carver to lead them. He became the first popularly elected, not appointed, governor in the history of English colonization. To guarantee that the governor was always the leader the colonists preferred, the Pilgrim Elders, or leaders, decided to hold an election every year.

Those who voted in the colony did not have to be Separatists. However, following English law, only men who owned property were eligible to vote. These voting members were known as freemen.

ESTABLISHING PLYMOUTH

The Compact in place, the colonists now had to find a site for their colony. The Pilgrims had anchored near present-day Provincetown. But fearing the harbor would not protect the *Mayflower* from the harsh winter weather to come, they widened their search. They explored up and down the coast. They waded through icy water and hiked miles through thick woods.

Once a group came upon six Native Americans with a dog. When the Native Americans ran into the forest, the Pilgrims lost sight of them. But they did find buried baskets of seed corn, which they gratefully took back to the ship. Food was always scarce.

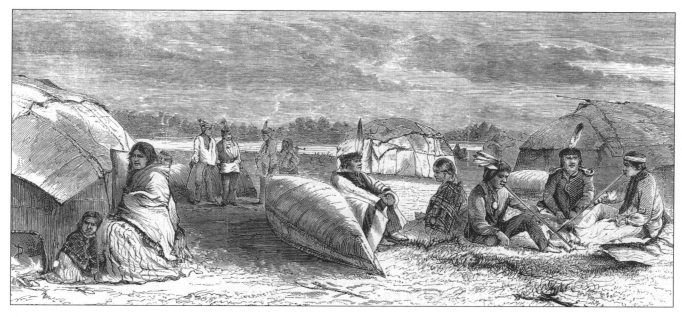

Many Native American cultures in the Northeast used saplings and bark for their houses.

After this encounter, the colonists did not see any more Native Americans, but they knew they were there. At night they heard them calling back and forth in the darkness. Some of their equipment mysteriously disappeared, and one day they came upon native houses. Built out of bent young trees and covered with bark, these dwellings were large enough to stand up in, and had fire pits for cooking.

A month later, a party of eight or nine Pilgrims walked into a deserted Native American village. There were no houses, but the land was cleared and there were abandoned cornfields nearby. Beneath the frozen surface, the dirt in these fields was rich and black, which meant the soil was good for farming. There were also freshwater streams close by, and the harbor was protected. The place looked promising.

★ ★ ★ ★

NAMING PLYMOUTH

In 1614 the English sea captain John Smith drew a map of the New England coast. The Native American village on Cape Cod Bay was named New Plymouth to honor the trading port of Plymouth, England. Eventually the name was shortened to Plymouth.

In 1607, before he explored the New England coast, John Smith helped found the English colony of Jamestown in Virginia.

The Pilgrims reviewed all the sites they had explored. They discussed the pros and cons of each without arguing. Bound by the Mayflower Compact, together they chose the deserted village they knew as Plymouth.

"THE GENERAL SICKNESS"

On December 12, 1620, the *Mayflower* sailed into Plymouth Harbor. Immediately, some of the men went ashore and started building the village. All other passengers stayed on the ship. By January 9, 1621, they had finished a common house, a 20-foot (6.1-m) square structure in which they stored materials from the ship. The house also provided shelter for the men while they built additional quarters.

The weather was often cold and rainy; the wind, icy. The Pilgrims, run-down from the voyage, worked constantly in wet clothing. Yet they did not stop, even when they came down with an illness they called the "general sickness."

This disease, which attacked the lungs, lingered on in the colony from January until mid-March. At one point there were only seven healthy people left to care for all the sick. Fifty-two people died: thirteen of the eighteen wives, nineteen of the twenty single men, and half the crew. Of the children, all seven girls lived, as did ten of the thirteen boys. Oceanus, whose birth on the *Mayflower* had been such a sign of hope, did not live through it.

The sickness was devastating, but the experience brought the Strangers and Separatists closer as a community. Together they suffered. Together they buried their dead. Together they survived.

Despite the harsh weather and the "general sickness" of that first winter, the Pilgrims did not give up.

By the end of March the Pilgrims had built six huts. It was now possible for the last of the *Mayflower* passengers to come ashore. On April 5, 1621, the ship sailed back to England. There was nothing in the hold for the investors, but no colonists went back either. Those who had survived the winter were committed to the new colony.

"WELCOME"

On March 16, 1621, the Elders were meeting in the common house. Suddenly a Native American appeared at the door. "Welcome, Englishmen," he said.

Samoset was the first Native American to contact the Pilgrims.

Upon hearing his words, the Pilgrims realized they were not as isolated as they had thought. If some Native Americans spoke English, the colonists would be able to communicate with the people who were their true neighbors.

Known as Samoset, this Native American was an Abenaki Sagamore. He had learned English from British fishermen who visited the Newfoundland coast. He explained that Plymouth was the Native American village Patuxet. Two thousand people had lived in the area until a deadly disease brought by European sailors swept through the community in 1618.

Six days after this first meeting, Samoset returned with Squanto. Also known as Tisquantum, Squanto was a Wampanoag and the only survivor of the Patuxet plague. Captured by the English and sold into slavery in Spain, he managed to escape back to England. Helped by a merchant, he too learned English before returning to New England with a French sea captain.

Squanto taught the Pilgrims how to plant corn, trap animals,

Many Pilgrims thought Squanto was sent by God to help them.

and tap maple trees for syrup. He introduced the Elders to the chiefs of nearby tribes. He was so helpful that Bradford described him as "a special instrument sent (by) God."

TREATY

Squanto also arranged for the Pilgrims to meet Massasoit, the leader of the Wampanoag. The Wampanoag, a confederation of several local tribes, were part of the Algonquian nation. They lived 40 miles (64 km) southwest of Plymouth on Narragansett Bay. When Massasoit came, he brought sixty men with him. He wanted to give the Pilgrims the message they were not welcome. In the past, too many Europeans had come with guns to kidnap Native Americans.

In the beginning Massasoit thought it was possible for Native Americans and Pilgrims to live in peace.

Samples of traditional objects from the Wampanoag culture still exist today.

When the Pilgrims arrived in 1620, Narragansett Bay was inhabited by the Wampanoag, even though the bay now has the name of the Narragansett tribe. Eventually, this Wampanoag land came under the control of the Plymouth Colony.

THE NARRAGANSETT AND THE PILGRIMS

Unlike the Wampanoag, the Narragansett never accepted the Pilgrims. In 1622 they sent them arrows wrapped in snakeskin to symbolize their desire to fight. The Pilgrims sent the skin back filled with bullets. Afraid of guns, the Narragansett backed down, but they always hated the English settlers.

Massasoit saw, however, that these English people were different. They came with their families. They told him they wanted peace. They offered gifts of soft cloth, metal tools, and copper. Massasoit agreed to talk. He thought that if the Wampanoag signed a treaty with the Pilgrims, the Pilgrims might protect them from their enemies, the Narragansett.

For their part, the Pilgrims wanted a treaty because they needed the Wampanoags' help. They had to be taught how to fish, hunt, plant, and harvest. They also needed to trade with the Wampanoag for beaver pelts to send back to the English investors.

Understanding the importance of cooperation, the Wampanoag and the Pilgrims agreed not to enter each other's villages with weapons. The Wampanoag returned the metal farming tools they had taken. The Pilgrims paid for the seed corn they had taken when they arrived. Each also consented to come to the other's defense if attacked.

HARVEST FESTIVAL

As summer went on, good weather and abundant crops improved the health of the Pilgrims. In mid-October, inviting the Wampanoag to join them, they held a secular, or nonreligious, three-day festival to celebrate

THANKSGIVING

For the Pilgrims a day of thanksgiving was a day to pray and thank God for His blessings. The original Harvest Festival of 1621 wasn't renamed Thanksgiving until 1863, when President Lincoln proclaimed the day a national holiday.

Recognizing how helpful the Wampanoag had been, the Pilgrims invited them to their feast which celebrated the colony's first good harvest.

Codfish and squash were staples of the Pilgrims' diet.

the harvest. Massasoit came with ninety Wampanoags. They brought venison, or deer meat, to add to the Pilgrim's table of roasted **fowl,** fish, vegetables, and fruit.

There were many differences between the Wampanoag and the Pilgrims. What kept them together were the harsh conditions in which they both lived. Both had to survive a hostile climate, unfriendly tribes, and the very real possibility of starvation. It was appropriate, therefore, that they celebrated their mutual good fortune together.

TROUBLE FROM ENGLAND

The colony's routine was disrupted on November 11, when the *Fortune* arrived from England with thirty-five more Separatists, but no supplies—no tools, nails, seed, oil, or clothing. Nothing. The ship did bring a letter from Thomas Weston. The letter stated that to get any support, the Pilgrims would have to sign the contract they had refused to sign before they left England. The Elders had no choice. They signed and sent goods such as **clapboard** and animal skins back with the *Fortune.*

The following summer, two more ships arrived with sixty men and another letter from Weston. Weston wrote that he had left the original investor group. "I am quit of you," he announced, "and you of me for that matter."

In fact, the Pilgrims weren't rid of him. In this same letter Weston asked them to take care of these men until they got settled. This was not easy to do. The Pilgrims were concerned they would not have enough food for themselves and these new arrivals over the next winter.

Nevertheless, in part because of their religious beliefs, the Elders did give the men some aid when they settled 40 miles (64 km) north in Wessagusset. Here they started a community whose only purpose was to trade with the Native Americans for goods to sell in England. From the beginning, the settlement struggled. The men did not farm properly. They fought and stole from each other. They treated the Native Americans with no respect.

The Pilgrims offered guidance based on their experiences. They suggested laws. They told the men how to make the most of the area's natural resources. They urged them to get along with the Native Americans. Weston's men did not listen.

In early spring, 1623, the Pilgrims heard that the Massachusetts tribe was going to attack Wessagusset. Afraid they would attack Plymouth next, the Elders sent Miles Standish and eight heavily armed men to the colony. In the end, at least three Massachusetts were killed, and the rest escaped into the woods. Most of Weston's men left New England. The Wessagusset colony had failed.

THE GENERAL COURT

Plymouth, on the other hand, prospered. The Pilgrims were committed to both their religion and their community. Therefore, they did everything they could to keep the community strong. To solve problems, the Elders established the General Court. Run by the governor and his elected assistants, this court made decisions and passed laws for the colony.

A skilled communicator, Edward Winslow was often sent to negotiate with local Native American tribes.

For example, the court decided to send Standish to Wessagusset because it felt the colony had to be protected. For the most part, however, the Pilgrims tried to keep peace with the Native Americans. When Massasoit was very ill, the court sent Edward Winslow to his village with medicine

Pilgrim children did not have easy childhoods.

THE CHILDREN OF PLYMOUTH

Pilgrim children were expected to help the community.

Younger ones ran errands, fetched wood and water,

and helped with the harvest. Older boys plowed fields.

Older girls cooked. All were brought up to become

responsible adult members of the colony.

to show the colony's concern. The medicine worked, and Massasoit recovered. As a result, the Wampanoag refused to join the Massachusetts when they turned against the English settlers.

Just because Plymouth had a working government did not mean that everything ran smoothly. Some settlers felt that others did not do their share of the work for the colony as a whole. To lessen the friction, the General Court gave each family its own acre of land to farm. To ensure equality, every year each family farmed a different acre. "The arrangement," Bradford wrote, had "a very good success." Because families could now keep some crops for themselves, "all hands [were] very industrious."

In July 1623 the *Anne* and the *Little James* brought ninety-three new Separatists to Plymouth. For the most part these new colonists settled in without problems.

By 1627, when the contract with the English investors ended, the General Court enacted new policies to strengthen all the colonists' commitment to Plymouth. One very important decision gave both voting and nonvoting settlers 20 acres (8.1 hectares) of land. The remaining land was held for those Separatists still to come.

The last sixty arrived in 1630 on the *Handmaid*. Each of these new colonists was given a house and provisions for sixteen months. The Mayflower Separatists had not forgotten their promise to provide for all the Separatists who came after them.

The Kennebec River marked the northernmost territory claimed by the Plymouth Colony.

THE GENERAL FUNDAMENTALS

The colony, which now consisted of approximately three hundred people, had grown physically as well. Its villages stretched from the Cohasset River to Narragansett Bay and included Cape Cod, both sides of Buzzards Bay, and a settlement on the Kennebec River in Maine.

With so many Pilgrims living outside of Plymouth, freemen had difficulty getting back to the General Court for meetings and elections. In 1636, therefore, the colony adopted the General Fundamentals. These new laws

Friction between the Native Americans and the English worsened as more colonists moved to New England.

THE IMPORTANCE OF EDUCATION

Separatists believed that everyone should read the Bible so that everyone could interpret God's word for himself or herself. Therefore, education was important in Plymouth. Initially, parents taught their children. By 1658 each town in the colony was required by law to have a schoolteacher.

allowed freemen living away from Plymouth to send representatives to vote in their place. The Fundamentals also stated that everyone, regardless of his or her status in the colony, was entitled to trial by jury. In addition, anyone on trial could object to a particular juror.

THE END OF THE TREATY

Throughout this period, other English settlers came to New England. The Puritans were one of the more well-known religious groups who came to practice their faith without fear. In 1630 seven hundred Puritans sailed into Massachusetts Bay on eleven ships. Unlike the Separatists, the Puritans had not wanted to break with the Church of England. However, they too believed that the Bible was the foundation of Christianity. They too were persecuted for their beliefs.

To all these settlers, New England was a vast uninhabited territory, full of promise. To the Native Americans who lived on the land, these settlers were intruders. The Native Americans may have tolerated the first small Pilgrim colony, but as more communities were built, that acceptance turned to anger. Conflict was inevitable.

In 1637, furious about trading posts in the Connecticut River Valley, the Pequot tribe attacked English settlements. The settlers fought back. Three weeks later, hundreds of settlers and Native Americans were dead, and the Pequot were destroyed.

When war finally broke out between the Pequots and the English, the Pequots were destroyed.

An uneasy truce, or pause in the fighting, lasted until 1675, when war broke out between the English and the Wampanoag. Massasoit's son, Metacomet, who was also known as King Philip, attacked Plymouth and other settlements throughout New England. Metacomet was enraged. The English had taken too much Wampanoag land. They had also insisted the Wampanoag become Christian and submit to their English law. The Pilgrims, who had come for religious freedom, did not understand that Native Americans wanted the same for their people.

ROGER WILLIAMS

Roger Williams, the founder of Rhode Island and a Protestant minister, supported the right of Native Americans to follow their own religions. He also declared that "King James (had) no more right to . . . sell Massasoit's lands . . . than Massasoit (had) the right to sell King James's kingdom."

Roger Williams (1603–1684) was an early voice for Native American rights.

His father had saved Massasoit's life, but Josiah Winslow would lead the colonial army against the Wampanoag people.

Metacomet, called King Philip by the English, was Massasoit's son. Believing there could be no peace because the English did not respect the rights of the Wampanoag, he went to war against the colonists.

The conflict, known as King Philip's War, lasted a year. In the end, Metacomet was killed, and the Wampanoag were defeated. It was Edward Winslow's son, Josiah, who led the English troops against his father's former allies. It is doubtful that either the Pilgrims or the Wampanoag thought their alliance would come to this bitter end.

It is doubtful too that the Pilgrims thought their colony would end. However, as more non-Separatists arrived, it became increasingly difficult for Plymouth to stay independent. In 1692 it merged with the Puritan Massachusetts Bay Colony. The General Court no longer met, but many of its self-governing policies were accepted by this larger, more financially successful colony.

The town meeting was a place where colonists could speak their mind.

BEYOND THE MAYFLOWER COMPACT

The Mayflower Compact also no longer exists as a working agreement. It was written at a specific time for a specific purpose—to help the Pilgrims establish their religious community. Outside the borders of Virginia Territory, thousands of miles away from king and country, these first colonists had to write their own laws.

These circumstances made the Mayflower Compact the first document written in the colonies that formulated rules for self-government. Other documents would follow. But because it was the first, the Mayflower Compact was both an important historical milestone and a stepping-stone to the future.

The Mayflower Compact ensured the rights of a small group of Protestant men in a small New England colony. Today, the United States **Constitution** ensures the rights of all U.S. citizens, regardless of their religion, gender, race, or ethnic background. The country has traveled far since that cold November morning in 1620.

THE TOWN MEETING

New England town meetings grew out of the General Court meetings held in Plymouth. Common throughout the eighteenth century, these meetings are still held today. They provide communities with a place to discuss and solve town problems.

Glossary

civil order—rules and laws relating to the nonreligious and nonmilitary code used by citizens of a community

clapboard—thin, narrow wooden board used as siding

colony—a community of people living in a separate territory from the parent country, but still tied to it

Constitution—the document that defines the laws of the United States and the structure of its government

denominations—religious groups that unite their congregations into a single body that shares similar beliefs

emigrate—to leave the country that one is in to settle somewhere else

fowl—large birds, such as geese or turkeys, found in the wild

natural resources—sources of wealth found in nature

New World—name given to North America and South
America by English and European settlers in the
seventeenth century

pelt—animal skin, with or without fur, hair, or wool

persecution—being harassed or attacked for one's beliefs

profit—money earned after the expenses of a business
have been paid off

sect—a religious group connected through shared beliefs
or leaders

sponsor—a person or organization that pays for, and is
responsible for, the activities of another person or
organization

trade—to exchange goods with another person or group

Timeline: The Mayflower

700 BC– AD 1,000	1534	1602	1606	1609	1614	1620

Early and Middle Woodland Period of Native American culture in New England during which the use of corn is introduced.

King Henry VIII breaks with the Roman Catholic Church and establishes the Anglican Church.

English sea captain Bartholomew Gosnold sails into Cape Cod Bay, giving both Cape Cod and Martha's Vineyard their English names.

The Separatists break away from the Church of England to start their own sect.

English Separatists flee England for Holland.

English sea captain John Smith draws a map of the New England coast.

The Mayflower sails for North America on September 6. The Mayflower Compact is written on November 9.

Compact

1621	1630	1636	1637	1646	1675	1692

1621 — The Pilgrims and the Wampanoag sign a treaty in the spring. They celebrate a Harvest Festival in October.

1630 — The last of the Separatists arrive on the *Handmaid*. The Puritans arrive in Massachusetts Bay.

1636 — The General Fundamentals are added to the General Court of the Plymouth Colony.

1637 — The Pequot attack English settlements, and three weeks later, following bloody battles, the Pequot are destroyed.

1646 — *Of Plimoth Plantation* by William Bradford is published.

1675 — King Philip's War ends the treaty between the Pilgrims and the Wampanoag.

1692 — The last meeting of Plymouth's General Court is held. The Plymouth Colony merges with the Massachusetts Bay Colony.

45

To Find Out More

BOOKS

Bradford, William. *Of Plymouth Plantation,* new ed. New York: A. A. Knopf, 2001.

Colby, Jean Poindexter. *Plimoth Plantation, Then and Now*. New York: Hastings House Publishers, 1970.

Hakim, Joy. *A History of Us, Making Thirteen Colonies*. New York: Oxford University Press, 1993.

Heaton, Vernonn. *The Mayflower*. Exeter, England: Webb & Bower Publishers, 1980.

Ziner, Feenie. *The Pilgrims and Plymouth Colony*. New York: American Heritage Publishing Co., Inc., Harper & Row, 1961.

ONLINE SITES

The Mayflower Society
www.mayflower.org

Plimoth-on-Web: Plimoth Plantation: The Living History Museum
http://www.plimoth.org

Index

About the Author

Melissa Whitcraft lives in Montclair, New Jersey, with her husband and their two sons. She has a Master of Arts in theatre. In addition to plays and poetry, she has written both fiction and nonfiction for children. She has published *Tales from One Street Over,* a chapter book for early elementary grade readers. Her biography, *Francis Scott Key, a Gentleman of Maryland,* was published as a Franklin Watts First Book. Ms. Whitcraft has written books on the Tigris and Euphrates, the Niagara, and the Hudson for the Watts Library series. She also wrote *Seward's Folly* for the Cornerstones of Freedom, Second Series.